The Essential

Points

For

Kendra Adachi

The Plan

Manage Your Time Like

A Lazy Genius.

Justty Rachy

TABLE OF CONTENTS

INTRODUCTION

CHAPTER 1
EMBRACE THE LAZY GENIUS WAY

CHAPTER 2
WHAT REALLY MATTERS – DISCOVERING YOUR
PRIORITIES

CHAPTER 3
TIME TO BE A GENIUS – CREATING YOUR LAZY
GENIUS SYSTEM

CHAPTER 4
FINDING YOUR FOCUS – DECLUTTERING YOUR
MIND

CHAPTER 5

THE ART OF SAYING NO – PROTECTING YOUR
TIME AND ENERGY

CHAPTER 6
THE POWER OF PRIORITIZATION – MAKING
CHOICES THAT MATTER

CHAPTER 7
THE ART OF DELEGATION – SHARING THE LOAD

CHAPTER 8
THE IMPORTANCE OF REFLECTION – LEARNING
FROM YOUR EXPERIENCES

CHAPTER 9
THE ROLE OF REST AND RENEWAL –
RECHARGING FOR SUCCESS

CHAPTER 10
THE POWER OF INTENTIONAL LIVING – CRAFTING
YOUR LIFE BY DESIGN

CONCLUSION

INTRODUCTION

In a fast-paced world full of distractions, demands, and competing priorities, it's easy to feel like life is happening to us rather than being shaped by us. We rush through our days, reacting to external pressures, often finding ourselves exhausted, unfulfilled, or disconnected from what we truly want. Our time, energy, and attention are consumed by responsibilities, social expectations, and the endless stream of tasks that demand our focus.

But what if it didn't have to be this way? What if we could take control of our lives, prioritize what truly matters, and create a path that leads to personal fulfillment and success? This book, "The Essential Points Of The Plan: Manage Your Time Like a Lazy Genius," offers a roadmap to help you do just that. It's about managing your time not through rigid schedules or relentless productivity hacks, but through intentional living – making conscious, deliberate choices that align with your values and goals.

Intentional living is more than just a time-management tool. It's about designing your life based on what you value most, rather than letting circumstances or societal expectations dictate your path. It's a way to ensure that your actions, whether big or small, contribute to the life you truly want to live. By focusing on what matters, you can eliminate the clutter – both mental and physical – that often stands in the way of genuine satisfaction and growth.

This book will show you how to break free from the cycle of mindless busyness. You'll learn how to manage your time in a way that serves your long-term vision, giving you more space to breathe, reflect, and enjoy the present moment. The techniques and strategies outlined in these pages aren't about squeezing more productivity out of your day. Instead, they are about empowering you to spend your time on what truly counts, so that every day feels meaningful and aligned with your greater purpose.

We'll dive deep into the art of identifying your core values, setting goals that align with them, and making intentional choices that bring you closer to the life you want. You'll discover practical tools to help you eliminate distractions, set healthy boundaries, and stay focused on what matters most. From learning how to rest and renew your energy, to building a supportive environment that fosters your growth, this book will guide you through each step of living intentionally.

Along the way, we'll also address the common challenges that arise, such as procrastination, overwhelm, and burnout. You'll gain insights into how to overcome these obstacles and stay on course, even when life gets hectic or stressful. The goal is not perfection but progress – finding a balance that works for you and allows you to live with greater clarity, purpose, and joy.

Whether you're someone who constantly feels overwhelmed by their to-do list, or you're searching for more meaning and satisfaction in your daily life, this book will offer practical, actionable advice to help you regain control. It's about helping you move from a life of reaction to a life of intention, where you are the architect of your own experience.

By the end of this journey, you'll have the tools and mindset needed to manage your time in a way that not only boosts your productivity but also enriches your life. You'll feel more connected to your purpose, more in control of your day-to-day choices, and more empowered to build a future that reflects your deepest desires.

So, let's embark on this journey together. It's time to stop letting life happen to you and start creating a life you truly love – one thoughtful, intentional choice at a time. Welcome to the path of intentional living.

CHAPTER 1

EMBRACE THE LAZY
GENIUS WAY

We all want to manage our time better, but most of us are exhausted from constantly feeling like we're not doing enough. Maybe you've tried countless productivity tips—waking up earlier, organizing every corner of your life, or using apps that promise to save you time. But even after all that, you still feel overwhelmed, and your to-do list never seems to shrink. What if there's a better way?

This is where the Lazy Genius approach comes in. It's not about working harder or finding some magical secret to squeezing more hours out of the day. It's about learning to be "lazy" about the things that don't matter and a "genius" about the things that do. This mindset frees you from the pressure of trying to do everything perfectly and allows you to focus on what actually makes a difference in your life.

What Does It Mean to Be a Lazy Genius?

The Lazy Genius approach is all about balance. It's not about being lazy in a negative way, where you ignore your responsibilities or let things fall apart. Instead, it's about being intentional with where you put your energy and attention. You don't need to hustle nonstop or perfect every detail of your life to be productive. In fact, that's what leads to burnout. The key is knowing what matters to you and being smart about those things while letting go of the rest.

Imagine you have a messy kitchen. You could spend hours organizing every drawer, making it Pinterest-worthy, but if what really matters to you is cooking healthy meals, then maybe your time is better spent on meal planning and keeping your fridge stocked. You don't need to stress about having a spotless kitchen if that's not what actually makes your life better.

The Problem with Trying to Do It All

The world constantly tells us we need to do more, be more, and achieve more. Social media shows us other people's perfectly curated lives, making us feel like we're falling behind. But the truth is, trying to do everything only leaves us exhausted and unsatisfied. When we try to juggle too many things at once, nothing gets the attention it deserves, and we end up feeling like we're failing on all fronts.

The Lazy Genius way teaches us that it's okay to let some things slide. It's okay to be "lazy" about certain tasks so you can be "genius" about the things that actually matter to you. This means you don't have to be great at everything—just the things that are important.

Start with What Matters

Before diving into time management techniques or productivity hacks, the first step is to figure out what really matters to you. This can be different for everyone. For some, it might be spending more time with family, for others, it might be pursuing a career goal, or even having more time for self-care.

Once you know what matters, you can start making decisions based on those priorities. Instead of doing more, you'll focus on doing the right things—the things that will bring you joy, peace, or progress. Everything else can take a backseat.

The Power of Letting Go

One of the most freeing parts of the Lazy Genius approach is letting go of the things that don't matter. Think about the areas of your life where you feel pressure to be perfect, but deep down, you know they aren't important. Maybe it's having the perfectly clean house, responding to every email immediately, or keeping up with every trend. The truth is, you don't need to be perfect in those areas if they're not part of what truly matters to you.

By letting go of unnecessary expectations, you're giving yourself permission to focus on what really counts. This not only reduces stress, but it also makes your efforts more meaningful. You'll feel less overwhelmed and more satisfied because you're investing your time and energy in things that actually matter.

The Lazy Genius Principle in Action

The beauty of the Lazy Genius mindset is that it's flexible. It adapts to your life, your goals, and your circumstances. You're the one in control. You get to decide what's worth your time and what isn't. This approach isn't about following someone else's strict rules for productivity—it's about creating a plan that works for you.

Throughout this book, we'll dive into practical strategies and simple routines that help you manage your time like a Lazy Genius. You'll learn how to create a system that fits your life, so you can stop feeling overwhelmed and start feeling in control.

Remember, it's not about doing it all. It's about doing what matters. So let's get started on this journey to smarter, more meaningful time management. You've got this!

1. What tasks or responsibilities in your life feel overwhelming, and how might you approach them differently by focusing on what truly matters to you?

_____

_____

_____

_____

_____

2. Can you think of a time when trying to do everything left you feeling exhausted? What could you have let go of to reduce that stress?

_____

_____

_____

_____

3. What are three priorities in your life that bring you joy or fulfillment? How can you make more time for them?

4. Are there any areas in your life where you feel pressured to be perfect but know deep down they aren't that important? How would letting go of those expectations change your daily life?

_____

_____

5. If you could choose just one thing to focus on in the next week that would make you feel more productive and satisfied, what would it be

_____

_____

_____

_____

_____

CHAPTER 2

WHAT REALLY MATTERS – DISCOVERING YOUR PRIORITIES

Managing your time effectively starts with a simple but powerful question: *What really matters to you?* In a world filled with distractions, endless tasks, and other people's expectations, it's easy to lose sight of what's truly important. But when you take the time to figure out what matters most, everything else starts to fall into place.

In this chapter, we're going to help you uncover your priorities. These are the things that deserve your time, energy, and focus. Once you identify them, you'll be able to filter out all the noise, making your life less overwhelming and more meaningful.

Why Priorities Matter

Think about how many times you've spent your day doing things that don't really move the needle. Whether it's mindlessly scrolling through social media, saying yes to obligations you don't enjoy, or wasting time on tasks that aren't essential, it's easy to get stuck in the cycle of busyness without real progress. That's where knowing your priorities comes in. When you're clear on what matters, you can make better decisions about where to invest your time.

Prioritizing helps you avoid the trap of doing *everything* and instead focus on doing the *right* things.

How to Identify Your Priorities

To figure out your priorities, ask yourself a few simple questions:

1. What brings you joy? These are activities, people, or experiences that light you up. They make you feel alive and fulfilled.

2. What brings you peace? These are the things that make your life easier and less stressful. It could be a routine, a space, or a relationship that provides stability.
3. What moves you closer to your goals? Whether personal or professional, these are the tasks and habits that help you grow, learn, or make progress towards the future you want.

Once you know your answers, you can start making choices based on what matters most. For example, if spending time with family is a top priority, you can let go of guilt when you turn down an invitation to work late. If reaching a fitness goal is important, you'll feel empowered to schedule time for exercise, even if it means saying no to other commitments.

The Trap of Urgency

One of the biggest challenges in managing time is that we often confuse *urgent* tasks with *important* ones. Urgent tasks demand our immediate attention but might not contribute much to our long-term goals. Important tasks, on the other hand, are the ones that align with your priorities and bring you closer to the life you want.

A simple way to tell the difference is to ask: *Will this matter in a week? A month? A year?* If the answer is no, it's probably not as important as it seems in the moment.

Setting Boundaries to Protect Your Priorities

Once you've identified what matters most, the next step is protecting your time for those things. This means setting boundaries—learning to say no to tasks, obligations, and distractions that don't align with your priorities.

Remember, every time you say yes to something that doesn't matter, you're saying no to something that does. Boundaries are about making space for the things that deserve your time.

Living in Alignment with Your Priorities

Life will always throw unexpected things your way. But when you're clear about your priorities, it becomes easier to adjust and keep your focus where it matters.

This doesn't mean your days will be perfect or stress-free, but you'll feel more in control, less overwhelmed, and more connected to what really matters.

In this chapter, we've taken the first step in managing your time like a Lazy Genius—getting clear on your priorities. With that clarity, you're ready to move forward with purpose and intention, knowing that you're building a life that reflects what truly matters to you.

1. What are three things in your daily life that truly bring you joy, and how much time are you currently dedicating to them?

_____

_____

_____

_____

_____

2. What are some activities or commitments that often feel urgent but don't actually align with your long-term goals? How can you start saying no to these?

_____

_____

_____

_____

3. Think about a recent day when you felt overwhelmed. What tasks or distractions took up your time, and were they aligned with your top priorities?

_____

_____

_____

4. If you could only focus on one priority in your life for the next month, what would it be and why?

5. What boundaries can you set right now to protect your time and energy for what truly matters to you?

CHAPTER 3

TIME TO BE A GENIUS – CREATING YOUR LAZY GENIUS SYSTEM

Now that you have a clearer idea of what truly matters in your life, it's time to build a system that helps you manage your time effectively. The goal here isn't to make you feel overwhelmed with more tasks or complicated plans. Instead, we'll focus on creating a Lazy Genius system tailored to your needs, one that allows you to maximize your productivity while keeping stress at bay.

Understanding Your Current Situation

To create an effective system, it's important first to understand how you currently manage your time. Take a moment to assess your daily habits. What works well for you, and what doesn't? Consider keeping a time log for a week, where you jot down how you spend each hour. This exercise can reveal patterns in your time usage and help you identify areas that need improvement.

Building Your Lazy Genius System

Creating a Lazy Genius system involves simplifying and organizing your approach to daily tasks. Here are some key strategies to help you develop your personalized system:

1. Prioritize Tasks: Start by listing everything you need to do. Then, categorize these tasks based on their importance and urgency. Focus first on the tasks that align with your core priorities. By concentrating on what truly matters, you'll reduce overwhelm and make progress toward your goals.

2. Time Blocking: This technique involves setting aside specific blocks of time for different activities. Instead of multitasking or constantly switching between tasks, dedicate uninterrupted time to focus on one thing at a time. For example, reserve a morning block for deep

work, another block for meetings, and time for personal projects or self-care.

3. Establish Routines: Routines can help automate parts of your day, making it easier to stick to your priorities. Consider developing a morning routine that energizes you for the day ahead, like exercising, meditating, or reviewing your goals. In the evening, create a wind-down routine to help you relax and reflect on your day.

4. Create a "Done" List: Instead of only focusing on what you need to accomplish, maintain a "done" list that captures everything you achieve each day. This practice reinforces a sense of accomplishment and helps you recognize your progress, no matter how small.

5. Streamline Decisions: Decision fatigue can hinder your productivity. To counter this, simplify your choices where possible. For example, plan your meals for the week in advance to save time each day. This not only eases your daily decision-making but also keeps you focused on your priorities.

Letting Go of Perfection

As you implement your Lazy Genius system, it's crucial to remember that perfection is not the objective. Life is unpredictable, and plans may not always go as intended. Instead of striving for perfection, aim for progress. Embrace the inevitable messiness of life and allow yourself to adapt as needed. Flexibility is an essential component of the Lazy Genius approach.

Staying Accountable

Accountability is a powerful tool in maintaining your new system. Share your goals and routines with someone you trust—be it a friend, family member, or colleague—who can encourage and support you along the way. Journaling about your experiences can also provide insights into what works and what doesn't, allowing you to fine-tune your system.

Visualizing Your Ideal Day

To further refine your Lazy Genius system, take some time to imagine your ideal day. What does it look like?

What tasks and activities fill your time, and how do you feel throughout the day? Use this vision as a guiding light when creating your routines and time blocks. Aligning your system with what you truly want will enhance your motivation to stick with it.

Embracing Your Unique Approach

Remember that there's no universal solution for managing time effectively. Your Lazy Genius system should reflect your personality, preferences, and lifestyle. Experiment with different strategies and tailor them to suit your needs. The ultimate goal is to create a system that feels effortless and sustainable, empowering you to enjoy your life while remaining productive.

As you embark on this journey to build your Lazy Genius system, keep in mind that it's a continuous process of learning and adapting. Embrace each step as an opportunity for growth, and trust that you're moving closer to a more balanced and fulfilling life. Let's work together to craft a system that helps you manage your time like a Lazy Genius, allowing you to focus on what truly matters!

1. What specific tasks or responsibilities in your daily life do you think deserve more focus, and how can you prioritize them effectively in your schedule?

_____

_____

_____

_____

2. How would implementing time blocking change the way you approach your daily activities? What types of tasks would you allocate specific time slots for?

_____

_____

_____

_____

_____

3. What elements of your current routines can you modify to help automate your day and make it easier to stick to your priorities?

_____

_____

_____

_____

_____

4. How can keeping a "done" list impact your motivation and sense of accomplishment? What small wins can you celebrate by tracking your progress?

_____

_____

_____

_____

_____

5. What decisions in your daily life could you simplify to reduce decision fatigue? How might planning ahead help you feel more organized and focused?

_____

_____

_____

_____

CHAPTER 4

FINDING YOUR FOCUS –
DECLUTTERING YOUR MIND

In our fast-paced world, distractions are everywhere. From notifications on our phones to endless to-do lists, it's easy to feel overwhelmed and lose focus on what truly matters. In this chapter, we will explore the importance of decluttering your mind and finding your focus so you can effectively manage your time and energy.

Understanding Mental Clutter

Mental clutter refers to the thoughts, worries, and distractions that can take up valuable mental space. This clutter can stem from unfinished tasks, worries about the future, or even the pressure to meet societal expectations. When your mind is cluttered, it becomes challenging to concentrate on the tasks that matter most to you. Recognizing this clutter is the first step toward finding clarity and focus.

Identifying Your Distractions

To declutter your mind, start by identifying your distractions. Take a moment to reflect on what tends to pull your attention away from your priorities. Are you often distracted by social media, emails, or notifications? Do you find yourself worrying about tasks that are not urgent but still linger in your mind? Write down the distractions you face regularly, and consider how they impact your ability to stay focused.

The Power of Mindfulness

One effective way to combat mental clutter is through mindfulness. Mindfulness involves being present in the moment and fully engaging with your current task. Practicing mindfulness can help you cultivate awareness of your thoughts and emotions, allowing you to manage distractions more effectively. Simple techniques like deep breathing, meditation, or even mindful walking can ground you and refocus your energy.

Setting Boundaries

Setting boundaries is crucial in maintaining focus and reducing mental clutter. Identify areas in your life where you can establish limits. This may involve designating specific times to check emails, turning off notifications during work periods, or setting aside time for self-care without interruptions. By creating boundaries, you protect your time and mental space, enabling you to concentrate on what matters most.

Prioritizing Your Tasks

Once you've decluttered your mind and set boundaries, it's time to prioritize your tasks effectively. Use the priorities you identified earlier to guide your focus. Break your tasks into manageable chunks and tackle them one at a time. This approach can help you maintain momentum and prevent feeling overwhelmed by the larger picture.

Embracing the Power of "No"

A significant aspect of decluttering your mind is learning to say "no" when necessary. It's easy to take on too many commitments out of obligation or fear of disappointing others. However, every new commitment adds to your mental load. Practice evaluating requests against your priorities and don't hesitate to decline those that do not align with your goals. Saying "no" can create space for the things that truly matter.

Creating a Focused Environment

Your environment plays a vital role in your ability to focus. Take a look around your workspace and consider whether it supports your productivity. Declutter your physical space by removing unnecessary items that can distract you. Consider organizing your workspace in a way that promotes concentration, such as having all your essential tools within reach and minimizing visual clutter.

Establishing Focus Rituals

Establishing rituals that signal it's time to focus can also help declutter your mind. These rituals can be as simple as a five-minute meditation before starting work, listening to specific music, or even enjoying a cup of tea. Find what works for you and make these rituals a regular part of your routine. They can help cue your brain to shift into a focused state.

Regular Reflection

Finally, make time for regular reflection on your mental clutter and focus. Set aside a few minutes each week to evaluate what's been working for you and what needs adjustment. Are there new distractions that have emerged? Have you been able to maintain your focus on what matters? This ongoing reflection will help you stay aligned with your goals and adjust your strategies as needed.

Decluttering your mind is a crucial step in the Lazy Genius approach. By reducing mental clutter, setting boundaries, and prioritizing tasks, you create an environment where focus can thrive. As you work through this process, remember that it's okay to seek support from others. Share your challenges and successes with friends or family who can encourage you along the way.

Finding your focus is an ongoing journey. It requires practice and commitment, but the rewards are worth it. As you declutter your mind, you'll find it easier to concentrate on what truly matters, allowing you to manage your time like a Lazy Genius and live a more fulfilling life.

1. What specific distractions in your daily life do you find most challenging to manage, and how do they impact your ability to focus on your priorities?

2. How can you incorporate mindfulness practices into your daily routine to help clear mental clutter and improve your focus?

_____

_____

_____

_____

_____

3. In what areas of your life do you struggle to set boundaries, and how might establishing limits help you create more mental space for important tasks?

_____

_____

_____

_____

4. Reflect on a recent situation where saying "no" could have helped you maintain your focus. What criteria will you use in the future to evaluate new commitments against your priorities?

_____

_____

_____

_____

5. What rituals or practices can you establish to signal to yourself that it's time to focus, and how might these routines enhance your productivity?

_____

_____

_____

CHAPTER 5

THE ART OF SAYING NO – PROTECTING YOUR TIME AND ENERGY

In a world where everyone seems to be vying for your attention, learning to say no is one of the most powerful skills you can develop. This chapter will explore why saying no is essential for managing your time and energy effectively, and how to do it with confidence and grace.

Understanding the Importance of Saying No

Saying no is not just about rejecting requests or opportunities; it's about prioritizing your time and energy for what truly matters to you. Every time you say yes to something that doesn't align with your goals, you risk spreading yourself too thin and diluting your focus. This can lead to burnout, stress, and ultimately a decrease in productivity. By saying no, you are making a conscious choice to protect your time and ensure that your energy is directed toward your most important tasks.

Recognizing Your Limits

To become comfortable with saying no, it's crucial to understand your limits. Take some time to reflect on what your boundaries are. What commitments do you currently have that feel overwhelming or unmanageable? By recognizing your limits, you can better evaluate new requests and determine whether they fit within your capacity. Remember that it's okay to have limitations; they are a natural part of being human.

Evaluating Requests

When faced with a request, pause and consider the following questions:

- Does this align with my priorities and goals?
- Will this commitment help me grow or contribute to my well-being?

- How will taking on this responsibility affect my current workload?
- Am I feeling pressured to say yes, or is this a genuine opportunity I want to pursue?

These questions can help you clarify whether a request is worth your time and energy. If it doesn't align with your priorities, it's perfectly acceptable to say no.

Practicing Assertiveness

Saying no can feel uncomfortable, especially if you fear disappointing others. However, practicing assertiveness can help you communicate your boundaries effectively. When you decline a request, do so with confidence and kindness. You don't need to provide lengthy explanations or justifications for your decision. A simple, direct response can be just as powerful. For example, you might say, "I appreciate you thinking of me, but I can't commit to that right now."

Creating a "No" Script

If you struggle with how to say no, consider developing a "no" script that you can use in different situations. This can be a simple phrase or a more detailed response that you feel comfortable with. For example, you could say, "Thank you for the invitation, but I have prior commitments that I need to honor." Having a prepared response can reduce anxiety and make it easier to assert your boundaries when needed.

Reframing Your Perspective

It's essential to reframe how you view saying no. Instead of seeing it as a negative action, think of it as an opportunity to say yes to your priorities. By declining a request, you create space for what truly matters in your life. This shift in perspective can help alleviate the guilt that often accompanies saying no.

Handling Guilt and Pressure

Even with the best intentions, saying no can still lead to feelings of guilt or pressure. It's important to acknowledge these feelings but not let them dictate your decisions. Remind yourself that prioritizing your time and energy is a form of self-care. Surround yourself with supportive people who respect your boundaries and encourage you to prioritize your well-being.

The Benefits of Saying No

When you practice saying no, you'll likely notice several positive outcomes in your life. You may experience reduced stress, increased focus on your priorities, and a greater sense of control over your time. Saying no also allows you to dedicate your energy to the commitments that genuinely matter, leading to more meaningful experiences and accomplishments.

Building a Supportive Network

Having a network of supportive friends, family, or colleagues can help reinforce your ability to say no. Surround yourself with people who understand the importance of setting boundaries and who will respect your decisions. Sharing your experiences and challenges with them can provide encouragement and accountability as you navigate this journey.

Saying no is not a selfish act; it's a necessary skill for anyone looking to manage their time effectively. By understanding your limits, evaluating requests thoughtfully, and practicing assertiveness, you can protect your time and energy for what truly matters. Embrace the art of saying no, and you'll find that it opens up new opportunities for growth and fulfillment in your life.

1. What specific situations or requests make you feel pressured to say yes, and how can you prepare yourself to respond assertively in those moments?

2. Reflect on a time when saying no positively impacted your life. What did you learn from that experience about the importance of prioritizing your time and energy?

_____

_____

_____

_____

3. How do your personal values and goals influence your decision to say no? In what ways can you better align your responses with these priorities?

_____

_____

_____

_____

4. What strategies can you implement to handle feelings of guilt when you decline a request? How can reframing your perspective help alleviate this guilt?

5. How can you build a support network that encourages healthy boundaries and respects your decisions to say no? What steps can you take to strengthen these relationships?

CHAPTER 6

THE POWER OF PRIORITIZATION – MAKING CHOICES THAT MATTER

In the hustle and bustle of everyday life, it's easy to feel overwhelmed by all the things you need to do. Prioritization is the key to navigating this chaos and ensuring that you're focusing your time and energy on what truly matters. In this chapter, we will explore how to effectively prioritize your tasks and commitments so you can lead a more balanced and fulfilling life.

Understanding Prioritization

At its core, prioritization is about making choices. It involves determining what is most important and deciding how to allocate your time accordingly. By prioritizing effectively, you can ensure that you're working on tasks that align with your values and goals, rather than getting bogged down by less important activities.

The Importance of Values

To prioritize effectively, you first need to understand your values. What is truly important to you? This could be family, career, health, personal growth, or community involvement. Take some time to reflect on your core values, as they will serve as your guiding principles when making decisions about how to spend your time.

Creating a Priority List

Once you've identified your values, the next step is to create a priority list. Write down all the tasks and commitments on your plate. Then, categorize them based on their importance and urgency. A common method is the Eisenhower Matrix, which divides tasks into four categories:

1. Urgent and Important: These tasks require immediate attention and should be done first.
2. Important but Not Urgent: Schedule time to complete these tasks; they are essential for long-term goals.
3. Urgent but Not Important: Delegate these tasks if possible, as they don't align with your core values.
4. Neither Urgent nor Important: Consider eliminating these tasks altogether.

By categorizing your tasks, you can quickly identify what needs your attention and what can be deprioritized or even removed from your list.

Setting SMART Goals

As you prioritize your tasks, it's helpful to set SMART goals—Specific, Measurable, Achievable, Relevant, and Time-bound. This framework can guide you in creating clear and attainable goals that align with your priorities. For example, instead of saying, "I want to get fit," a SMART goal would be, "I will exercise for 30 minutes, three times a week, for the next month." Setting specific goals gives you a clearer roadmap to follow.

Learning to Let Go

Part of effective prioritization is recognizing that you can't do everything. There will always be more tasks and commitments than you have time for. It's important to let go of activities that don't align with your priorities or values. This might mean declining invitations, stepping back from certain responsibilities, or even saying goodbye to old habits that no longer serve you. Embracing this mindset can free up time and energy for what truly matters.

Regularly Reassessing Your Priorities

Priorities can change over time as your circumstances, goals, and values evolve. Therefore, it's crucial to regularly reassess your priorities and make adjustments as needed. Set aside time each week or month to reflect on your current commitments. Are they still aligned with your goals? Do they continue to serve your values? This ongoing assessment will help you stay focused on what's important.

Using Tools to Aid Prioritization

There are various tools and techniques that can assist you in prioritizing your tasks. Whether it's a digital app, a planner, or even a simple notepad, find a method that works best for you. Use color coding, symbols, or checklists to visually organize your tasks. The goal is to create a system that makes it easy for you to see what needs to be done and what can wait.

Balancing Short-term and Long-term Goals

Effective prioritization involves balancing short-term tasks with long-term goals. While it's essential to address urgent matters, don't lose sight of your bigger objectives. Make sure to allocate time for activities that contribute to your long-term aspirations, even if they don't seem urgent. This balance will help you stay on track and prevent you from getting caught up in a cycle of reacting to immediate demands.

Seeking Support

Finally, don't hesitate to seek support from others in your prioritization process. Share your goals and commitments with friends, family, or colleagues who can offer guidance and encouragement. They can help hold you accountable and provide valuable perspectives on what's truly important.

In summary, the power of prioritization lies in making intentional choices about how you spend your time. By understanding your values, creating a priority list, and setting SMART goals, you can focus on what matters most. Remember, it's okay to let go of tasks that don't serve your priorities and to reassess your commitments regularly. With effective prioritization, you'll find that you can manage your time like a Lazy Genius and live a more balanced, fulfilling life.

1. What are your core values, and how do they influence the way you prioritize your tasks and commitments in daily life

_____

_____

_____

_____

_____

2. Using the Eisenhower Matrix, how would you categorize your current tasks? What steps can you take to address tasks that are important but not urgent?

_____

_____

_____

_____

_____

3. Reflect on a recent goal you set for yourself. Was it specific, measurable, achievable, relevant, and time-bound? How can you apply the SMART criteria to future goals for better results?

_____

_____

_____

_____

_____

4. What tasks or commitments have you been holding onto that no longer align with your priorities? How can you begin to let go of these responsibilities?

_____

_____

_____

_____

_____

5. How often do you reassess your priorities, and what process do you use to evaluate whether your current commitments still align with your goals and values?

CHAPTER 7

THE ART OF DELEGATION – SHARING THE LOAD

In our journey to manage time effectively, one crucial skill that often gets overlooked is delegation. Many people struggle with the idea of letting go of tasks, believing that they must do everything themselves to ensure it gets done right. However, learning to delegate can be a game changer, allowing you to free up your time, reduce stress, and empower others in your life. In this chapter, we'll explore the art of delegation and how it can enhance your time management skills.

Understanding Delegation

At its core, delegation is about entrusting responsibilities to others. It's recognizing that you don't have to do everything alone and that there are capable individuals who can share the load. Whether at work, home, or in your community, effective delegation can help you focus on your priorities while empowering others to contribute their skills and talents.

Identifying Tasks to Delegate

The first step in effective delegation is identifying which tasks can be delegated. Not all tasks are suitable for delegation, so consider the following criteria:

1. Time-Consuming Tasks: If a task takes a significant amount of your time and could be done by someone else, it may be worth delegating.

2. Tasks That Don't Require Your Expertise: Are there tasks that don't require your specific skills or knowledge? These are often prime candidates for delegation.

3. Repetitive or Routine Tasks: Tasks that are repetitive and don't require much thought can be delegated to free up your time for more strategic activities.

4. Opportunities for Others to Grow: If you have team members or family members who could benefit from taking on new responsibilities, consider delegating tasks that can help them develop their skills.

Choosing the Right Person

Once you've identified tasks to delegate, the next step is choosing the right person for each responsibility. Consider the strengths, skills, and interests of those around you. Match the task to someone who has the capability or the willingness to learn. Effective delegation not only ensures that the task gets done but also allows others to grow and contribute to the team or family dynamic.

Communicating Clearly

Clear communication is essential for successful delegation. When you delegate a task, provide specific instructions about what needs to be done, including deadlines and expectations. Be open to questions and encourage the person you're delegating to reach out if they need clarification. This helps ensure everyone is on the same page and minimizes the risk of misunderstandings.

Trusting the Process

One of the biggest hurdles in delegation is the fear that things won't be done correctly. It's essential to trust the person you're delegating to and give them the autonomy to complete the task in their way. While it's natural to want to oversee everything, micromanaging can undermine the very benefits of delegation. Allow others the freedom to approach tasks in their unique way, which can often lead to innovative solutions.

Providing Support and Feedback

Delegation doesn't end with handing off a task. It's important to provide ongoing support and feedback. Check in periodically to see how the person is progressing and offer assistance if needed. Constructive feedback is also vital; it helps others improve and reinforces positive behaviors. Celebrate successes and acknowledge the effort put into the task, reinforcing their contributions and building confidence.

Learning to Let Go

Learning to delegate requires a mindset shift. It's about recognizing that you can achieve more by sharing the load. This means letting go of the idea that you must be in control of everything. Embrace the fact that delegation is not a sign of weakness but a strength that allows you to focus on your priorities while enabling others to shine.

Reassessing and Adjusting

After delegating tasks, take the time to reassess the process. Reflect on what went well and what could be improved. Did the person you delegated to feel supported? Were the tasks completed on time and to your standards? This reflection will help you refine your delegation skills over time, making you more effective in managing your responsibilities.

The Benefits of Delegation

When done correctly, delegation has numerous benefits. It frees up your time to focus on high-priority tasks, reduces stress, and fosters collaboration. Additionally, it empowers others to take on responsibilities, leading to personal growth and increased confidence. By embracing delegation, you create a more efficient and harmonious environment, whether at work or at home.

In conclusion, mastering the art of delegation is a powerful tool in your time management toolkit. By identifying tasks to delegate, choosing the right people, communicating clearly, and providing support, you can share the load effectively. Embrace the mindset of collaboration, and you'll find that delegation not only enhances your productivity but also strengthens relationships and fosters a sense of teamwork.

1. What tasks in your personal or professional life do you currently handle that could be delegated to others, and what criteria will you use to decide which tasks to pass on?

_____

_____

2. Reflect on a time when you successfully delegated a task. What challenges did you face, and what did you learn from that experience about trusting others?

_____

_____

_____

_____

_____

3. How can you identify individuals in your life or workplace who are well-suited to take on delegated tasks? What strengths or skills should you consider in your decision-making process?

_____

_____

_____

_____

_____

4. What fears or concerns do you have about delegating tasks, and how might addressing these feelings help you become more effective in your delegation efforts?

_____

_____

_____

_____

_____

5. After delegating a task, what strategies can you implement to provide constructive feedback and support

while allowing the person to maintain their autonomy?

_____

_____

_____

_____

_____

CHAPTER 8

THE IMPORTANCE OF REFLECTION – LEARNING FROM YOUR EXPERIENCES

In the fast-paced world we live in, it's easy to get caught up in the hustle and bustle of daily tasks and responsibilities. We often move from one obligation to the next without taking a moment to pause aand reflect on our experiences. However, reflection is a powerful tool that can enhance your time management skills and overall well-being. In this chapter, we will explore the importance of reflection, how to incorporate it into your routine, and the benefits it brings to your life.

Understanding Reflection

Reflection is the process of looking back on your experiences, thoughts, and feelings to gain insight and understanding. It allows you to evaluate what worked well, what didn't, and how you can improve moving forward. By taking the time to reflect, you can identify patterns in your behavior, understand your motivations, and learn from both successes and failures.

The Benefits of Reflection

Engaging in regular reflection has numerous benefits, including:

1. Increased Self-Awareness: Reflection helps you understand your strengths, weaknesses, and emotional responses. This self-awareness is crucial for personal growth and effective decision-making.

2. Enhanced Problem-Solving: By analyzing past experiences, you can identify what strategies were effective and what could be improved. This knowledge equips you with better tools for tackling future challenges.

3. Improved Time Management: Reflecting on how you spend your time allows you to identify areas where you

can be more efficient. You can discover tasks that drain your energy or activities that don't align with your priorities.

4. Goal Alignment: Regular reflection helps you stay connected to your goals and values. By assessing your progress, you can make adjustments to ensure you are on track toward achieving what truly matters to you.

Incorporating Reflection into Your Routine

To reap the benefits of reflection, it's essential to make it a regular part of your routine. Here are some practical strategies to help you integrate reflection into your life:

1. Set Aside Time: Dedicate a specific time each week or month for reflection. This could be as simple as a quiet moment with a journal or a structured session where you evaluate your progress on goals.

2. Ask Reflective Questions: Use guiding questions to prompt your reflections. For example:
   - What were my biggest accomplishments this week?
   - What challenges did I face, and how did I respond?

- How did my actions align with my values and goals?

- What lessons did I learn that I can apply in the future?

3. Keep a Reflection Journal: Writing down your thoughts can help clarify your insights and provide a record of your progress. Consider creating a dedicated journal where you can regularly document your reflections.

4. Seek Feedback: Engaging with others can enhance your reflective process. Seek feedback from trusted friends, family, or colleagues. Their perspectives can provide valuable insights and help you see situations from different angles.

5. Practice Mindfulness: Incorporating mindfulness techniques, such as meditation or deep breathing, can help you create a calm space for reflection. These practices can enhance your ability to be present and engage fully with your thoughts.

Learning from Your Experiences

As you reflect on your experiences, it's essential to adopt a growth mindset. Embrace the idea that failures and challenges are opportunities for learning and growth. Instead of dwelling on mistakes, focus on what you can take away from them and how you can apply these lessons moving forward. This mindset shift can empower you to approach challenges with resilience and adaptability.

Celebrating Successes

In addition to analyzing challenges, don't forget to celebrate your successes. Acknowledging your achievements, no matter how small, can boost your motivation and reinforce positive behaviors. Take time to recognize what you've accomplished and how far you've come on your journey.

Adjusting Your Approach

Reflection is not just about looking back; it's also about making adjustments for the future. After evaluating your experiences, consider what changes you can implement in your routines, habits, or strategies. Whether it's adjusting your time management techniques, altering your goals, or refining your delegation skills, use reflection as a guide for continuous improvement.

Creating a Reflective Culture

If you work in a team or community, fostering a culture of reflection can enhance collective growth. Encourage open discussions about successes and challenges, and create opportunities for team members to share their insights. This collaborative approach can lead to increased engagement, innovation, and a stronger sense of connection among team members.

In conclusion, reflection is a vital aspect of managing your time effectively and living a fulfilling life. By taking the time to assess your experiences, you can increase your self-awareness, improve your problem-solving skills, and align your actions with your goals. Make reflection a regular practice in your life, and you will discover its transformative power in helping you navigate challenges and celebrate successes. Embrace the journey of reflection, and watch as it enhances your personal and professional growth.

1. What specific techniques or methods can you incorporate into your routine to make reflection a regular practice in your life, and how do you envision this impacting your overall time management?

_____

_____

_____

_____

_____

2. Reflect on a recent challenge you faced. What did you learn from that experience, and how can you apply those lessons to similar situations in the future?

_____

_____

_____

_____

_____

3. How does self-awareness influence your ability to manage your time effectively? In what ways can increasing your self-awareness lead to better decision-making and goal alignment?

_____

_____

_____

_____

_____

4. Identify a recent success you achieved. What factors contributed to that success, and how can you celebrate or build on that achievement moving forward?

_____

_____

5. How can you create a culture of reflection in your team or community? What steps can you take to encourage open discussions about successes and challenges among your peers?

CHAPTER 9

THE ROLE OF REST AND RENEWAL – RECHARGING FOR SUCCESS

In our busy lives, we often equate productivity with constant activity. We push ourselves to accomplish more and more, believing that the harder we work, the more successful we will be. However, this mindset can lead to burnout and decreased effectiveness over time. In this chapter, we'll explore the crucial role of rest and renewal in managing your time and energy, and how taking breaks can enhance your overall performance and well-being.

Understanding Rest and Renewal

Rest is not merely the absence of work; it is a vital component of a healthy and productive life. Just as machines need downtime to function optimally, our bodies and minds require rest to recharge and rejuvenate. Renewal involves engaging in activities that replenish your energy, creativity, and motivation. Together, rest and renewal create a balanced approach to managing your time and responsibilities.

The Importance of Taking Breaks

Taking regular breaks throughout your day is essential for maintaining focus and productivity. Research has shown that working for extended periods without rest can lead to diminishing returns, where your effectiveness decreases as fatigue sets in. Short breaks can help improve concentration, creativity, and problem-solving abilities.

Consider incorporating techniques like the Pomodoro Technique, which involves working for a set period (e.g., 25 minutes) followed by a short break (e.g., 5 minutes). This structured approach encourages focused work while allowing for regular intervals of rest.

Prioritizing Sleep

One of the most critical aspects of rest is sleep. Sleep plays a vital role in cognitive function, emotional regulation, and overall health. Lack of quality sleep can lead to decreased productivity, impaired decision-making, and increased stress levels. Prioritize getting enough restorative sleep each night to ensure you wake up refreshed and ready to tackle the day.

To improve your sleep quality, establish a consistent sleep schedule, create a calming bedtime routine, and limit exposure to screens before bedtime. A well-rested mind is more capable of focusing and making sound decisions.

Incorporating Renewal Activities

Renewal activities are those that rejuvenate your spirit and creativity. These can vary widely from person to person, but some common examples include:

1. Physical Activity: Engaging in regular exercise can boost your energy levels, improve mood, and enhance

overall well-being. Whether it's a brisk walk, yoga, or hitting the gym, find a form of movement that you enjoy.

2. Creative Pursuits: Activities such as painting, writing, or playing music can foster creativity and provide an outlet for self-expression. Make time for hobbies that inspire you and bring joy.

3. Nature Breaks: Spending time in nature can have a profound impact on your mental health. Take a walk in the park, go for a hike, or simply sit outside and enjoy the fresh air. Nature can help clear your mind and restore your sense of calm.

4. Mindfulness Practices: Incorporating mindfulness techniques, such as meditation or deep breathing, can help reduce stress and enhance your focus. These practices encourage present-moment awareness and can improve your overall mental clarity.

5. Social Connections: Spending time with friends and loved ones can be rejuvenating. Nurturing relationships fosters a sense of belonging and support, which can boost your overall mood and resilience.

Recognizing Burnout

Burnout occurs when you feel physically, emotionally, and mentally exhausted due to prolonged stress or overwork. Symptoms may include chronic fatigue, irritability, decreased motivation, and a sense of detachment. It's essential to recognize the signs of burnout and take proactive steps to address it.

If you find yourself feeling overwhelmed, take a step back and assess your workload. Consider implementing more rest and renewal activities into your routine. It may also be helpful to seek support from friends, family, or mental health professionals.

Building a Culture of Rest

If you're in a leadership position or part of a team, consider fostering a culture that values rest and renewal. Encourage your team members to prioritize their well-being by promoting regular breaks, flexible work hours, and wellness initiatives. When individuals feel supported in their need for rest, overall productivity and morale improve.

The Long-Term Benefits of Rest and Renewal

Incorporating rest and renewal into your life can lead to long-term benefits, including improved mental clarity, increased creativity, enhanced problem-solving abilities, and a greater sense of fulfillment. When you take care of your mind and body, you set yourself up for sustainable success.

In conclusion, rest and renewal are vital components of effective time management and overall well-being. By prioritizing breaks, quality sleep, and activities that rejuvenate you, you can enhance your productivity and enjoy a more balanced life. Embrace the importance of rest, and you will find that taking time to recharge not only benefits you but also allows you to show up as your best self in all areas of your life.

1. What specific rest and renewal activities do you currently engage in, and how can you expand or improve these practices to enhance your overall

well-being and productivity?

_____

_____

_____

_____

_____

2. Reflect on a time when you experienced burnout. What signs did you notice, and what steps could you have taken to prevent it or address it more effectively?

_____

_____

_____

_____

_____

3. How does your current sleep routine impact your daily performance and overall mood? What changes can you make to prioritize better sleep quality in your life?

_____

_____

_____

_____

_____

4. What are some creative or physical activities that bring you joy and help you recharge? How can you integrate these activities into your regular schedule to ensure you are consistently renewing your energy?

_____

_____

_____

_____

5. If you were to build a culture of rest and renewal in your workplace or community, what policies or practices would you implement to support individuals in prioritizing their well-being?

CHAPTER 10

THE POWER OF INTENTIONAL LIVING – CRAFTING YOUR LIFE BY DESIGN

In a world filled with distractions and demands, it's easy to lose sight of what truly matters to us. We often find ourselves reacting to life's pressures rather than living intentionally according to our values and goals. This chapter delves into the concept of intentional living, exploring how to take control of your life, make purposeful choices, and create a life that reflects your true desires.

Understanding Intentional Living

Intentional living is about making conscious choices that align with your core values, beliefs, and goals. It involves being proactive rather than reactive, setting clear intentions for how you want to spend your time and energy. When you live intentionally, you create a life that feels authentic and fulfilling, rather than one shaped by external expectations or circumstances.

Defining Your Values and Goals

To live intentionally, you first need to identify your core values and goals. Reflect on what matters most to you in various aspects of your life, including your career, relationships, health, and personal growth. Consider the following questions to help clarify your values:

1. What principles guide your decisions and actions?
2. What brings you joy and fulfilment?
3. What do you want to achieve in the short term and long term?

Once you have a clear understanding of your values, you can set specific goals that align with them. Ensure that your goals are meaningful and resonate with your aspirations. This alignment will provide you with a sense of purpose and direction in your daily life.

Creating a Vision for Your Life

With your values and goals in mind, it's time to craft a vision for your life. Your vision should encompass the kind of life you want to lead, the experiences you want to have, and the person you aspire to become. Consider writing a personal mission statement that encapsulates your vision and serves as a guiding star for your decision-making.

Visualising your ideal life can also be a powerful tool. Create a vision board or use visualization techniques to picture yourself living out your goals and values. This practice can reinforce your intentions and motivate you to take action toward your vision.

Making Intentional Choices

Living intentionally requires making choices that align with your vision and values. Here are some strategies to help you make more deliberate choices in your daily life:

1. Prioritise Your Time: Evaluate how you spend your time each day. Are your activities aligned with your values and goals? Identify tasks that drain your energy or distract you from what truly matters, and consider delegating or eliminating them.

2. Set Boundaries: Establish clear boundaries to protect your time and energy. Learn to say no to commitments that do not align with your values or goals. Setting boundaries can empower you to focus on what is most important and prevent overwhelm.

3. Practice Mindfulness: Being present in the moment allows you to make more conscious choices. Mindfulness techniques, such as meditation or deep breathing, can help you become more aware of your thoughts and feelings, enabling you to respond intentionally rather than reactively.

4. Reflect Regularly: Set aside time for regular reflection on your choices and their alignment with your values and goals. This practice can help you assess your

progress and make necessary adjustments to stay on track.

Embracing Change and Growth

Living intentionally also means being open to change and growth. Life is dynamic, and your values and goals may evolve over time. Embrace the idea that it's okay to reassess your priorities and make adjustments as needed. This flexibility allows you to adapt to new circumstances while staying true to your core values.

Cultivating a Supportive Environment

Creating a supportive environment is crucial for fostering intentional living. Surround yourself with people who inspire and uplift you. Share your goals and values with your friends and family, and seek their support in your journey. Building a network of like-minded individuals can help you stay accountable and motivated.

The Benefits of Intentional Living

The journey of intentional living can lead to profound benefits, including:

1. Increased Fulfillment: When you align your actions with your values, you experience greater satisfaction and fulfillment in your life.

2. Improved Decision-Making: Intentional living provides a framework for making choices that resonate with your goals, leading to more effective decision-making.

3. Enhanced Resilience: By living with intention, you cultivate a sense of purpose that can help you navigate challenges with greater resilience and adaptability.

4. Stronger Relationships: When you prioritize what matters most to you, you can cultivate deeper and more meaningful connections with others who share your values.

In conclusion, intentional living is a powerful approach to managing your time and shaping your life. By defining your values, setting clear goals, and making conscious choices, you can create a life that reflects your true desires. Embrace the power of intention, and watch as you transform your daily experiences into a fulfilling journey that aligns with your vision for your life. Living intentionally empowers you to take control of your destiny and create a life by design rather than by default.

1. What are your top three core values, and how do they influence your daily decisions and actions?

_____

_____

_____

_____

_____

2. Reflect on a goal you set for yourself recently. How aligned is this goal with your values, and what steps can you take to ensure that you remain focused on achieving it?

_____

_____

_____

_____

_____

3. Describe your vision for your ideal life. What experiences, relationships, and achievements would it include, and how can you begin to incorporate elements of this vision into your daily routine?

_____

_____

_____

_____

_____

4. Identify a recent situation where you reacted rather than responded intentionally. What strategies can you implement to cultivate a more mindful and deliberate approach in similar situations in the future?

_____

_____

_____

_____

_____

5. How can you create a supportive environment that fosters your journey toward intentional living? What changes can you make in your relationships or surroundings to better align with your goals and values?

_____

_____

_____

CONCLUSION

As we wrap up our look at intentional living, it's important to see just how much our choices and mindset shape our lives. Living intentionally isn't just about managing time better; it's about making sure our lives reflect what we truly value and want. By identifying what matters most to us, creating a clear vision for our future, and making conscious choices, we give ourselves the power to lead a life that's meaningful and fulfilling.

In a world that constantly demands our attention, embracing intentional living acts as a compass, helping us navigate challenges with clarity. It reminds us that our time is limited and every moment is an opportunity to focus on what truly counts.

As you start this journey, remember that living with intention is not about being perfect. It's about making choices that align with your true self. Take time to reflect on your experiences, rest when you need to, and surround yourself with people who support your goals.

Living intentionally is about stepping into your power and designing a life that reflects who you really are. It helps you find balance in the chaos, prioritize your well-being, and nurture your relationships. As you apply these ideas in your everyday life, you'll see that every decision, no matter how small, adds up to the bigger picture of your life.

So take a moment, breathe, and move forward with confidence. Embrace the idea of intentional living, and watch how it helps you create a life that not only meets your dreams but also inspires others around you. The path may not always be clear, but with intention guiding you, every step can lead to a richer, more meaningful life. Your story is in your hands, and the best time to start is now.

Made in the USA
Columbia, SC
23 November 2024

47408333R00054